First World War
and Army of Occupation
War Diary
France, Belgium and Germany

66 DIVISION
198 Infantry Brigade
Prince of Wales's Leinster Regiment (Royal Canadians)
6th Battalion
1 June 1918 - 16 September 1918

WO95/3140/5

The Naval & Military Press Ltd
www.nmarchive.com
Published in association with The National Archives

Published by

The Naval & Military Press Ltd

Unit 10 Ridgewood Industrial Park,

Uckfield, East Sussex,

TN22 5QE England

Tel: +44 (0) 1825 749494

www.naval-military-press.com

www.nmarchive.com

This diary has been reprinted in facsimile from the original. Any imperfections are inevitably reproduced and the quality may fall short of modern type and cartographic standards.

© **Crown Copyright**
Images reproduced by permission of The National Archives, London, England, 2015.

Contents

Document type	Place/Title	Date From	Date To
Heading	WO95/3140/5		
Heading	66th Division 198th Infy Bde 6th Bn Leinster Regt 1918 Jun-1918 Sep From E.G.J.P.T 10 Div 29 Bde Disbanded		
Heading	66th Division 198 Infy Bde 6th Bn Leinster Regt Jun 1918		
Heading	War Diary of 6th Btn The Leinster Regt From June 1st To June 30th 1918 Vol No XXXIV		
War Diary	At Sea	01/06/1918	01/06/1918
War Diary	Marseilles	01/06/1918	04/06/1918
War Diary	In Train	05/06/1918	07/06/1918
War Diary	Aire	07/06/1918	08/06/1918
War Diary	La Roupie	09/06/1918	17/06/1918
War Diary	On Move	18/06/1918	18/06/1918
War Diary	Wicquinghem	19/06/1918	29/06/1918
War Diary	Serqueux	30/06/1918	30/06/1918
Miscellaneous	6th (Ser) Bttn Leinster Regt Increase and decrease Table for the month of June 1918	01/07/1918	01/07/1918
Heading	War Diary of 6th (S) Bn Leinster Regiment From 1st July 1918 To 31st July 1918 Volume No. XXXV		
War Diary	Abancourt	06/07/1918	31/07/1918
War Diary	Serqueux	01/07/1918	04/07/1918
War Diary	Abancourt	05/07/1918	05/07/1918
Miscellaneous	6th Leinster Regiment Increase And Decrease Table For Month Of July 1918	01/08/1918	01/08/1918
Heading	War Diary of 6th (S) Bn Leinster Regiment From 1-8-18 To 31-8-18 Volume XXXVII		
War Diary	Abancourt	01/08/1918	31/08/1918
Miscellaneous	Bttn Leinster Regt	31/08/1918	31/08/1918
Heading	War Diary of 6th (S) Bn Leinster Regt From 1.9.18 To 16.9.18 Volume No.37		
War Diary	Abancourt	01/09/1918	16/09/1918

WO 95/3140/5

66TH DIVISION
198TH INFY BDE

6TH BN LEINSTER REGT.
~~JLY-SEP 1918~~

1918 JUN — 1918 SEP

FROM EGYPT - 10 DIV 29 BDE

DISBANDED

66/198

~~30TH~~ DIVISION
~~103RD~~ INFY BDE

6TH BN LEINSTER REGT
JUN 1918

FROM EGYPT

DISBANDED SEP 18

3028

2689

103/34

Vol 1

CONFIDENTIAL

WAR DIARY

OF

6TH BTN THE LEINSTER REGT

FROM JUNE 1ST TO JUNE 30TH 1916

VOL No XXXIV

WAR DIARY or INTELLIGENCE SUMMARY

Army Form C. 2118

6TH LEINSTER REGT
JUNE 1916
Sheet I
VOL XXXIV

Place	Date	Hour	Summary of Events and Information	Remarks and references to Appendices
At Sea	1/6		Arrived in dock early morning. Proceeding to disembark. Sheds for loading & unloading kept. Started to disembark at 11.45.	A/4
Marseilles			Every Coy in turn disembarkation completed by 12.10. Started to march to B.10 and camp at Musat. Very good road. Coys got in good time was last in thus. QM arrived in camp at 4.40 P.M. and Coys. at 6.0 in addition.	
	2/6		First day in clearing up men had rest all day. Passes issued to 10% of the men to go into Marseilles. Men were very fit after the trip.	left
"	3/6		Spent day in inspecting all Coy O.C. Red Cross kits – inspection. Passes issued to 10%. Received orders for station entraining.	left
	4/6		Marched from 11.10 Rest Camp to Point L to entrain. 4th entrained at 10.30. Train notice expected 12.60 n.	left

WAR DIARY or INTELLIGENCE SUMMARY.

Army Form C. 2118.

6TH LEINSTER REGT
JUNE 1916.
VOL. XXIV

Place	Date	Hour	Summary of Events and Information	Remarks and references to Appendices
In train	5/6/16		Had tea for good during night about 12.30 midnight men had tea which was already made when train arrived at station. Halt lasted about 45 minutes.	
"	6/6/16		Had hot dinner also for mid. Fra. service early when Fra. women of stations called held hands out, train blew at innumerable stations on this way back to Germany for overseas. Kill had a civil & merry reception.	
			Arrived at AIRE at 07.30. Marched to camp which men had to pitch tents very new place. Tents did not go up till afternoon. Camp situated a about 1½ miles E of AIRE. Glorious hot sun & showers came in 2 lots E of about ½ hour. Thought the men looked very fit with the camp. Tough, just went to us. 5th O.P. camped just next to us.	
AIRE	8/6/16		Paid to 16 DIV + 47 D. All day settling down for field cooker was contained fitted to those that & moved small camp not known & when	

WAR DIARY
INTELLIGENCE SUMMARY

6TH LEINSTER REGT
JUNE 1918
VOL XXXIV   Sht III

Army Form C.2118

Place	Date	Hour	Summary of Events and Information	Remarks and references to Appendices
LA ROUPIE	9/6/18		C.O. & Major Townshend went round line. Battalion not fighting to take 96 miles to earth for lectures, gas helmets & nose by gas chamber all helmets pattern with new containers. Bth Band opened practices commenced	
"	10/6/18		C.O. gave men lee. P.T. & Bayonet fighting class started, school from D/s Lieut. Gpl aimed to see foundation of season. Enemy started shelling town for reports etc. A.B & C. B'is went to watterin afternoon. Football match in evening Bth v Bth School. Bth won 4 nil	
"	11/6/18		P.T. & Bayonet fighting class during day. D.L. & H.Q. went to bath finishing at 11.00. C.O. went to Brench rd Div H.Q. and to gen commander Eurphia visit of Corps Commander at lunch turn was each B.G. by itself, several very pleasant and the look of the men.	
"	12/6/18		C.O. started work on trenches deft B'th arr at 07.15 shown out with them returning about 3.30 PM to 3.30 PM B.O. to Aust munitenance during morning & afternoon to see D.O. artillery 2/L WILLIAMS admitted to 1.F.A. Field Gardens came a cost to paying out close arrangements made for filly advance new from steepen field bathin B'th won B nil Football B'th v Bth School	

WAR DIARY
or
INTELLIGENCE SUMMARY.

(Erase heading not required.)

Army Form C. 2118

6th LEINSTER REGT

JUNE 1917

Vol XXIV Sheet IV

Place	Date	Hour	Summary of Events and Information	Remarks and references to Appendices
LA ROUPIE	13/6/17		C.O. went round line & visited working parties. C.O. 2nd Royal Irish Rifles informed Capt. H. Murphy on returning. Received orders from Bde warning to be ready to move. Took over new sector of line.	ELH
"	14/6/17		C.O. & many 3 officers advance drawn by Capt S.H. Monaghan in morning. C.O. paid visit in evening.	ELH
"	15/6/17		Received orders to move on 17th inst to VERCHOCQ via WANDONNE & DENNEBROEUCQ when Btn will stop for two nights in billets.	ELH
"	16/6/17		C.O. finished work at 12.00 orders in main outline. 8th to march to RADINGHEM. Later the night these orders made out. Capt EWENS U S.A.M.O. took over.	ELH
"	17/6/17	09.00	Btn moved off at 09.00. Lt DALTON sent off to WIGQOINGHEM and later Lt HORTON went on by lorry to RADINGHEM to get billets for Btn. Officers billets were very bad, Btn arrived at RADINGHEM at 7.30 P.M. very long march.	ELH

WAR DIARY or INTELLIGENCE SUMMARY.

(Erase heading not required.)

6TH LEINSTER REGT
JUNE 1916
Army Form C. 2118
VOL XXXIV

Place	Date	Hour	Summary of Events and Information	Remarks and references to Appendices
On March	18/6/16		18th left RADINGHEM at 10-0AM. Lt HORTON went on in lorry to WIEQINGHEM to arrange billets, good billets for men & officers. 18th arrived at WIEQINGHEM at 5-30 PM. By 8 all settled down in billets by 7.0 PM	R.L.B.
WIEQINGHEM	19/6/16		C.O. went round & inspected all billets. DA.Q.M.G. 34 DIV came to see C.O. about allotment for 18th in place. C.O. went round with Major of village to settle better field for open inspection to take place on 20-6-16	R.L.B.
"	20/6/16	12-10 AM	Wet morning, half of day DIV Gen inspected 18th at 12-10 AM, men left off wild evening until 2th & brought was Cpt Lt in charge. New arrivals Lt Col O.B. Slacum or Huntley and Lt. C.F. Smyth, Lt W.S. Bayne & Lt F.M. Gaunt. G#Q Medical officer came to inspect all men & send to staff Gunner every day. Anwyen wish Major to have field for training, REs came to erect small mill. Would not get field for training. All Planchets at 8 pm and up to be Wieqinghem	R.L.B.
	21/6/16			R.L.B.

WAR DIARY or INTELLIGENCE SUMMARY.

6th LEINSTER REGt Army Form C. 2118

JUNE 1918
VOL XXXIV

Place	Date	Hour	Summary of Events and Information	Remarks and references to Appendices
WIEQUINGHEM	22/6/18		Fatigue party to leave Liffre hut at 6-AM 7hrs. of marching. 4 men to go every day. D.I.V Sig. Officer came to see B.C. asked to hand B.O. I went round to see all billets.	WJB
"	23/6/18		Church parade. R.C. 8.0AM in village church. C.of E. at 10.45AM in School Supers. D.I.V. Band played for two hours. 11-12 orderly Quarter. 12-1 Lunch. Arrangements made to form field Library. Lt J.E.O. Mullin on Comttee. 2/Lt Gordon on T.M. exam.	WJB
			Exam. Lt J.E. Dalton M.C. Lt J.E.O. Mullin on Comttee. 2/Lt Gordon on T.M. exam.	
"	24/6/18		Walks started on 70yds range & border ground marching. From 9 to 12 & 1 to 4 two different parties for each day. L.T.B. to W. Fifth range at QUESLIN (St. Millis) followed by Majority to B.& 2 R.W.H. Gasborne & D.S.O. HORTON went with first party at 9. Magority attested as follows: 2/Lt Murphy, 2/Lt Ennis, 2/Lt O'Mullin to see Boundary ground Ranges on Boundary.	WJB
"	25/6/18		DIV. General was heard in morning, went up to see G.O.C. Boundary ground. We all go forced out. Two Lewis Guns to take turns over to SAMER to arrive in evening. 20 men gave tea & B.G. advance party got back about 10-11PM	WJB

WAR DIARY or INTELLIGENCE SUMMARY

Army Form C. 2118
6th LEINSTER REGT.
JUNE 1918
Vol XXXIV

Place	Date	Hour	Summary of Events and Information	Remarks and references to Appendices
WICQUING-HEM	26/6/18		Received orders to move on 27th entraining at DESVRES for ROMESCAMPS. Unable to procure C.O. shot in left leg by Pte McDonald who was drunk. C.O. sent to Ft. in evening. Have put off moved train at 11.00 PM. Major J.S. TOWNSHEND M.C. took over command of Btn.	
	27/6/18		In orders of move yet. 6th Ewens returns to Btn. Orders for move received at midnight. B Coy to entrain at DESVRES at 6 PM & Coy A SERQUEUX. Lt Baron reported from Lucerne & sent with on loan to UK. Lt W Wicquinghem at LENNIS went on loan to UK. Lt W Wicquinghem at 9.0 AM.	
	28/6/18		B Coy moved out of WICQUINGHEM at 1 PM to march to DESVRES Road. BOURTHES - FAUCHELLES - SACRIQUIER. B Coy entrained at DESVRES for SERQUEUX, arriving at DEVRES from WICQUING HEM at 4.15 PM. Train left DEVRES at 6.10 PM.	
	29/6/18		Btn arrived SERQUEUX at 9.0 AM arrived at camp about 1k mile from station at 11.0 AM. Men went off very well. Camp at SERQUEUX good.	

WAR DIARY or INTELLIGENCE SUMMARY.

6TH LEINSTER REGT
Army Form C.
Sheet VIII
JUNE 1918
VOL XXXIV

Place	Date	Hour	Summary of Events and Information	Remarks and references to Appendices
SERQUEUX	30/6/18		6 outs & Engineers tied to day on the car for the shooting of Sgt Wll Brooks Royal Irish Regt Match Officers B in 1 - Officer 14. Y.M.C.A opened in V.B. hutch R.C. Parade at 8.0 A.M. No C.of E parade L.T.R. camp. Pickup went on leave to U.K. train left SERQUEUX at 7.20 P.M.	W.R

2/6/18

J.A Hutton
a/Adjt
6th Leinster R

6th.(Ser.) Bttn. Leinster Regt.

Increase and decrease table for the month of June 1918.

Increase.	O.	OR'S.	Decrease.	O.	O.R'S.
Joined Bttn. from) Base Depot.)	4.	-	Sick to Hospital.	3.	331.
Rejoined from Hospital		19.	Struck off strength) Left in EGYPT.)	1.	18.
			Died in Hospital) from sickness.)	-	2.
	4.	19.		4.	351

Nett decrease. — 328.

1.7.18.

Vol III

CONFIDENTIAL.

198/66

WAR DIARY

OF

6TH (S) BN LEINSTER REGIMENT.

From 1st July. 1918.   To 31st July. 1918.

Volume No XXXV

WAR DIARY
or
INTELLIGENCE SUMMARY.
(Erase heading not required.)

6TH LEINSTER REGT Army Form C. 2118.
JULY 1916 Sheet II
VOL XXXV

Place	Date	Hour	Summary of Events and Information	Remarks and references to Appendices
ABANCOURT	6/7/16		Lt BARSON went to HAVRE to get all Rank Rets. 7.15am left at 8.0am in morning. Very hot during day.	
"	7/7/16		R.C. parade & C of E held close to camp. Guest just came in evening. 1 Officer, other parts in from & camp, very good.	
"	8/7/16		Lt FUDGER departed for duty, the morning walked from ROMESCAMPS arrived about 7.10am. Lt PHILLIPS went on leave to U.K. left ABANCOURT at 6.30pm.	
"	9/7/16		A, B & C.Coy bathed at BLARGIES. H.Q. and transport went and B.Q. Plenny all day except Quinain from stakes at 11.0am which 18th had 1/2 parade.	
"	10/7/16		G.O.C. 50 DIV visited camp. seemed very interested with things in travel. 8th Batd disembaptory & party to go down. D.B & went to huts at BLARGIES.	
"	11/7/16		Capt Monoghan went in two days leave to ROUEN. Leave not though. Capt Monoghan returned to camp in evening. Inspecting Capt EWENS. R/V 13th Lt McCAFFREY to own as M.O.	

WAR DIARY
or
INTELLIGENCE SUMMARY.
(Erase heading not required.)

6TH LEINSTER REGT Army Form C. 2118.
JULY 1916.
Vol XXXV
Sheet II

Place	Date	Hour	Summary of Events and Information	Remarks and references to Appendices
BLANGOURT	12/7/16		Capt Monaghan went on leave to ROUEN. General representative went up to PARIS from this Camp. Marched off about 5.0 AM. Football match between A+B Coy & C+D Coy, D.+C. Wd.	GHQ
"	13/7/16		2Lt CARSON returned from ROUEN and bombets. Football Hostel between Officers Nos 1, Nos 4, Officers Wd. ball found 4 hour before time. Pte PETRI went on leave to U.K. left about 7.0 PM.	GHQ
"	14/7/16		RC parade at 8.0 AM. Col. G.fE paraded at 8 LARGES at 10.0 AM. Football match between 5th & 5th Bn. Rangers. 5th Bn Rangers left. match stopped 10 minutes before time owing to Army border inspecting all troops at 6.0 PM. 6 Lt LEWIS returned from leave to U.K.	GHQ
"	15/7/16		Football match between 5th & 2/20 LONDON Regt. 5th 3- 2/20 LONDON 2. Lt Monaghan returned from leave to ROUEN. Thunder storm through night.	GHQ
"	16/7/16		Capt T.V. Powell returned to 5th from hospital, posted to B. Coy. Very hot all day.	GHQ

WAR DIARY
or
INTELLIGENCE SUMMARY.
(Erase heading not required.)

Army Form C. 2118

6TH LEINSTER REGT
July 1918
Chap IV
Vol XXV

Place	Date	Hour	Summary of Events and Information	Remarks and references to Appendices
ABANCOURT	17/7/18		Court Martial held on Pte McDonnell at ABANCOURT Camp H.Q. Enemy from 10 AM to 4.0 P.M. Very heavy Thunder storm in evening, tents etc blown down.	6L#
"	18/7/18		2/Lt Flavin returned from Hospital. Showing all day, camp in very muddy condition.	6L#
"	19/7/18		Major J.D. JOHNSTONE, LT. P. ST J. KELLEHER, M.C. Captain F.T.M. JONES, Lt. C.J. THORNTON, F. O'NEILL, H.T. WHITTAKER, D.A. McEVOY, E.A.Y. MASON with 84 O.R. joined the Bn from Base Depot. KANTARA. Lt. G.S. HORTON to U.K. on leave. R.G.C. 198 I.Bde visited Battn today, as Bn being holds that bde.	R
"	20/7/18		Major Johnstone assumed command of Bn today. Training from 6 am to 11 am and 1 pm to 3 pm. P.T. Leading of arms, Bath parade Manchester at 1 pm subject:- Gas drill, bayonet fighting. Bn team beats 1-0. Instructions received that Bn is now under 66th Divn and posted to 198th I.Bde. Lieut. H. WARBURTON rejoined from leave U.K. Divine Service for R.C's held in village church LANNOY-CUILLERE. C.H.E. in camp. 2nd Lt C.F. SMYTH to U.K. on leave. Capt. F. JONES took over command of D Coy from Capt H.E. Bruce.	R
"	21/7/18		Training continued. 11 O.R. rejoined from Battalion.	R
"	22/7/18		Training continued. Assumes command of Battalion. Lt. E.R. SCOTT to U.K. on leave. Lt KELLEHER in charge of Batta Transport. 2nd Lt. C.J. THORNTON took over duties of Signal Officer today from Lt P.T. ROE. Lt Roe posted to D Coy for duty.	R

WAR DIARY or INTELLIGENCE SUMMARY

Army Form C. 2118.

6 LEINSTER REGT
JULY 1918
VOL. XXXV
Sheet V

Place	Date	Hour	Summary of Events and Information	Remarks and references to Appendices
ABANCOURT	23/7/18		Coys attending lectures on gas by the Anti Gas instructor in Y.M.C.A. marquee at hours intimated from 9am to 12 noon. Rain falling from 8am to 10.15 prevented training being carried on. For parading dads at 11am for quinine (liquid) 15 grs. Since 9th instant marked improvement in health, malaria apparently yielding to treatment. During the afternoon the Bn and Coy Sgt Majs NCO's were lectured in accoutrements to S.B.R. drill under the Anti Gas instructor. Lt Mullins reported from leave to unit.	JR
—	24/7/18		Coys bathing at BLARGIES today. Training continuing when not at baths. C.O. (Major J.D. JOHNSTONE) attended a conference at 199 Inf. Bde. Hd Qrs. at 1am. Training, equipment, supply question were dealt with.	JR
—	25/7/18	9am	Battalion moved camp from No 3 area to No 1 area. Lieut H.T. Phillips rejoined from leave and resumed duties of TM Officer. 2/Lt WILLIAMS with Cpls HAMBLETON & BOND attending short course of instr- -ruction in Intelligence duties under Bde Intell. Officer. 8 N.C.O's commenced a course of P.T. + B.F. today under an instructor sent by Bde H.Q.	JR
—	26/7/18		Bn furnishing Camp duties today and bathing at Blargies.	JR

Army Form C. 2118.
Sheet VI

WAR DIARY
6 LEINSTER Regt
INTELLIGENCE SUMMARY.
JULY 1918
VOL XXXV

(Erase heading not required.)

Place	Date	Hour	Summary of Events and Information	Remarks and references to Appendices
ABANCOURT	27/7/18		Battn. fell into march, but owing to heavy rain, had to be cancelled. 30 yds range allotted to Battn. today. All Lewis guns put into action, and all such trained gunners received also all available men of C & D Coys put through rapid firing and rapid loading a range. Major T.B. Johnston proceeded on leave to U.K. for 14 days. Special allotment. The B.G.C. mailed the Bn lights & discovered minor defects.	R
—	28/7/18		Divine service for R.C.s held at church in LANNOY CUILLERES. C.of.E. service in the hutts of 5 R. Innis Fus. War Economists & Y.M.C.A. Lecturers during to 2 Coys of Bastin, all Coys were indirectly inspected by the P.O.C. today. Major T.S. Trombold, M.C. Comdg. Bn during absence on leave of Major Johnston.	R
—	29/7/18		Training continued. 1 officer (2/Lt. ATHERTON) and the B.L.G. S.M. (Sgt. HUNT) attending 2 day course of instruction in the "forward" men A.A. Sight & Lewis gun. From 6.30 am to 12.30 pm the Battn. is considered to be in the "Precaution ing Zone" for Gas defence. S.B.R's being worn by all ranks except ordinal staff & certain officers from 10 to 10.30 am. 29 O.R. admitted to hospital today with Scabies as a result of medical inspection yesterday. 2/Lt. T. Casson to U.K. on leave.	R

WAR DIARY
or
INTELLIGENCE SUMMARY.
(Erase heading not required.)

Army Form C. 2118.

6 LEINSTER Regt.
JULY 1918.
Vol. XXXV Sheet VII

Instructions regarding War Diaries and Intelligence Summaries are contained in F.S. Regs., Part II. and the Staff Manual respectively. Title pages will be prepared in manuscript.

Place	Date	Hour	Summary of Events and Information	Remarks and references to Appendices
ABANCOURT	30/7/18		Lt A.V. Petri rejoins from leave to U.K. Bn paraded at 6 a.m. for route march. 6½ miles, returning at 11.30. No casualties. Box respirators carried from 6.30 to 12.30 p.m. & with gas from 10 am to 10.15 a.m. B.G.S. inspected Bn Transport today at 11 a.m. Turn out very good. 2nd Lt L. ATHERTON appointed Bn Lewis gun officer vice Lt A.V. Petri posted to A Coy for duty.	AR
—	31/7/18		Bn furnishing camp guards, duties, and working parties as usual. Clothing of men inspected with reference put through the Trench disinfector. A & B Coys bathing at BLARGIES. C.O. with Coy Cmdrs reconnoitring ground near VALERY for a platoon Cmdrs scheme. A cross country race was held this afternoon by 4 battns. of the Bde — distance about 4 miles. The Bn team secured third place, which is gratifying as the Bn has not had any previous practice in cross country running. The health of the Bn has improved and is directly due to the general treatment lately, which is rapidly improved. Behaviour of the men to date very good. Weather & decision statement for month.	Appx I

Monaghan Capt.
6 Leinster Regt.

WAR DIARY or INTELLIGENCE SUMMARY

Army Form C. 2118.

6TH LEINSTER REGT
JULY 1916
Vol XXXV Sheet I

Place	Date	Hour	Summary of Events and Information	Remarks and references to Appendices
SERQUEUX	1/7/16		Field Cashier came up to 51st G.R. camp to pay out. B Coy money was drawn. Ldg. Serg Jon Tun was picked up. Also duplicate for April.	
"	2/7/16		B.Th Gaunt woking party to Officer (Lt Ennis) & 90 O.R. 40 to work under the Officer at Station, unloading trucks. 40 at Common work up cinema in camp. Went order to orderly officer YMCA put up. Rec'd verbal order to move to ABANCOURT on 4th inst. arrived in sidings that Regt would move to ABANCOURT joined 15th to day parties to R.G.S. 2/Lt ATHERTON joined	
"	3/7/16		Lt GAUNT Lt MULLINS 2/Lt STAINES & 2/Lt SMYTH admitted to hospital. Lt DALTON & 2/Lt BAGNAL returned to Bn from courses.	
"	4/7/16		Regt marched off from SERQUEUX at 0900 AM for ABANCOURT via LE THIL GAILLEFONTAINE PIERREMONT GRIQUEIAS. arriving at camp about 12 Kilos from ABANCOURT at 0400 PM camp attack fielded.	
ABANCOURT	5/7/16		Every body killed down in camp. Trucks for Bn rations commenced. 1 to 1 John Far Laid practice alarm at 0100 AM to man the rooms.	

(A7092) Wt. W1230/M295 750,000. 1/17. D.D. & L. Ltd. Forms/C2118/14

WAR DIARY.
6th Leinster Regiment.

Appx I

Increase and Decrease table for month of JULY 1918.

INCREASE.	O.	OR.	DECREASE.	O.	OR.
Joined Battn. from hospital.		212	Sick to hospital	3.	77
Joined Battn. from Base.	3.	3	Posted to Com. Bgde.	1.	--
			Trans. to R.Dub.Fus.		1
Total.	11.	215.	Total.	4.	78.
Nett increase.			6.	137.	

1.8.18

J. Monaghan Capt
Adj: 6 Leinster Regt.

WD 4 198/66

CONFIDENTIAL

WAR DIARY

of

6th (S). Bn. LEINSTER REGIMENT.

VOLUME XXXVII

From 1-8-18.   To 31-8-18.

WAR DIARY 6 LEINSTER REGT.
INTELLIGENCE SUMMARY. AUGUST 1918.
VOL. XXXVI   Sheet I

Army Form C. 2118.

Place	Date	Hour	Summary of Events and Information	Remarks and references to Appendices
ABANCOURT	1/8/18		C & D Coys with Council of A & B Coys falling in at BLARGIES in morning. Captain W.G. Cogin (Qr Mr) having proceeded on leave to UK last night. 2nd Lt W.S. Bagnall assumed duties of Acting Qr Mr today. Individual training continued in afternoon. At 4 pm all officers, W.Os & Sergeants attended a lecture by the Earl of Denbigh on "German War Aims" – the lecture being very instructive and brought home to all ranks the seriousness of the war. The A.D.M.S. 66 DIVN visited the lines during the afternoon & brought notice some few points to be remedied. Gas Alarm sounded at 10.30 and 11.45 when all ranks wore Box respirators for 15 minutes.	R
	2/8/18		Rain falling steadily during morning. Rain prevented practice for allotted 30 yds rifle range today but rain prevented practice until 11.30. Each Coy was allotted 1½ hours a range. At 3 pm the B.Q.C. delivered a lecture on "Changes in tactics" during the war, to all officers, W.Os and Sergeants. The general feeling was that although many new factors had been introduced, the general principles were still there in vogue before the war and that all training must be based on it. Lecture lasted for 65 minutes. Whilst D Coy were firing on the rifle range about 5.30 pm 2 men (7395 L/C Cary J and 9414 Pte Hayes M) were slightly wounded owing to a flash back afterwards, where Pte Hayes was firing – a portion of the bolt had blown off & striking the 2 men. Wounds slight and did not necessitate being sent to hospital.	R

Army Form C. 2118.

WAR DIARY or INTELLIGENCE SUMMARY.

2 LEINSTER REGT. AUGUST 1918.

Vol. XXXVI Sheet I

(Erase heading not required.)

Instructions regarding War Diaries and Intelligence Summaries are contained in F. S. Regs., Part II. and the Staff Manual respectively. Title pages will be prepared in manuscript.

Place	Date	Hour	Summary of Events and Information	Remarks and references to Appendices
ABANCOURT	2/8/18		Rain falling at intervals during afternoon and evening.	SR
—	3/8/18		Rain falling steadily during morning. Reconnaissance exercise for Platoon Comdrs. carried out today under Captain F. JONES. Capt. H.E. BRUCE to U.K. on leave.	SR
—	4/8/18		Brigade service (C. of E.) held today for Special Prayers at 10 a.m. R.Cs. at LANNOY Church at 10 a.m. Non Conformists at 10 a.m. in Y.M.C.A. During afternoon work carried out with tents, sinking floors bivouac 2 feet as protection against air raids.	SR
—	5/8/18		Lt. G.T. HOLM reported from leave U.K. at 5 a.m. Bn. on duty today; also bathing at BLARGIES in the morning. Vermorin men sent disinfectors at THRESH disinfector. Bn. Lewis Gunners training under Lt. WILLIAMS; Snipers, Scouts & 4 men per Coy commenced training under Lt. WILLIAMS. Intelligence duties. Reconnaissance scheme for Platoon Commanders was held during the afternoon, heavy rain however caused this training to be shortened.	SR
"	6/8/18		Short range adapted to B.R. today. A & B.Coy during morning. Snipers under the I.O. (Lt. WILLIAMS) from 12 noon to 2 p.m. C & D. Coy for remainder of afternoon. Bayonet fighting training for C & D during morning, A & B during afternoon.	SR

WAR DIARY or INTELLIGENCE SUMMARY

Army Form C. 2118.

6th LEINSTER REGT
AUGUST 1916
VOL XXXVII Sheet III

Place	Date	Hour	Summary of Events and Information	Remarks and references to Appendices
ABANCOURT	6/8/16		Football ground accepted to B'tn for drill during day. Rain fell during whole day.	
"	7/8/16		66th DIV Commander inspected B'tn the morning at 11.30 AM in marching order on hill on Western side of camp. B'tn was drawn up in Mass facing South, after inspection the General spoke to all officers individually. Platoon Commanders & N.C.Os in afternoon undergoing exercise work. Scheme of "U" in GOURCHELLE (shut to DIEPPE) at 3 P.M. Relieved Lapsed discussion of situation attacking enemy, then all day 2nd Lt J Powell went on leave to U.K. in evening	
"	8/8/16		Individual training for all day during morning. Organised war dogs away. 6.2" to .60 nights firing on range after lunch. B'tn Bomber played 24 London on 26 London ON DIV of Generals inspection large crowd march hast. 40 24 London to night, 26 Regt Lt Dalton M.C. to evident while party to go off to B.E.F. as far as Boulogne. Firm all day. Party of 1/98? 3 unable to go	
"	9/8/16		A B.2 on long range during morning B'tn on P.T. & games together. Bath for all known on range owing to lecture for B'tn in afternoon by Flight Col Campbell D.S.O on P.T. & games together. Battn for of known cancelled. Fine all day.	

WAR DIARY
or
INTELLIGENCE SUMMARY.
(Erase heading not required.)

Army Form C. 2118.

6TH LEINSTER REGT
AUGUST 1915.
Chap IV
VOL XXXVII

Place	Date	Hour	Summary of Events and Information	Remarks and references to Appendices
ADANCOURT	10/8/15		Bath found all Camp Duties to-day. B¹ⁿ attached Dumfries to-day. (6TH DIV Commander inspected transport of B¹ⁿ at 12·00 noon to-day. Officers who were in messing under Capt Jones — Road maintenance, LANNOY–CUILLIERE (sheet 16 DIEPPE). 11 N.C.O.'s moved to 15th from Bom. Rept.	ELB
—	11/8/15		Divine Services C. of E at 9·30, R.C. at 9·30 held in LANNOY. Lecture on aeroplanes by Fr Col James McRae in YMCA tent at 8·0pm. B¹ⁿ v 3rd London, London 1st B¹ⁿ won football match between B¹ⁿ v 3rd London, London 1st B¹ⁿ won	ELB
—	12/8/15		B¹ⁿ on Battalion training. A & B Co on High Ground N.W. of Camp 8, C & D Co on High Ground N.E. of Camp Any range allotted to C & D Co. A & C Co on night firing chart Range allotted to R & D Co. B¹ⁿ played football against 6th Lincs Reg, half.	ELB
—	13/8/15		9en Commanding 66th DIV gave lecture to B¹ⁿ at 11·15 AM Issue 9en Commanding 6 Bde Battery at BLARGIES. 2 Fr Infantry Returns 50 yds range. B¹ⁿ then UK on Room Route at BLARGIES allotted to D¹ⁿ during morning C of D Co's parade at A & B Co. bombing ground, allotted to	ELB
—	14/8/15		D & C Co's morning Regimt Sighting ground allotted to D. C & A Co afternoon. A. B. Co formed all Camp Duties	

WAR DIARY or INTELLIGENCE SUMMARY

Army Form C. 2118

LEINSTER REGT
AUGUST 1918
VOL XXXVII

Place	Date	Hour	Summary of Events and Information	Remarks and references to Appendices
ALANCOURT	14/8/18		Major B.J. JONES D.S.O. took over command of Bttn this morning. Major T. STOWNSHEND. M.C. to 2nd in Command. Return to Bn Y. Anti Gas Instructors on 30 yds range from 4.30 p.m. to 6.30 p.m. Bowen at Y.M.C.A. gave a lecture. Church Party in evening. Church Parade.	GWA
"	15/8/18		Football ground deepened to Btn for drill in morning. B+C Coy Lewis Gun + Lewis Gun for D+A Coys with Lewis Guns during morning. B+C.Coy + Lewis Gun during afternoon. Lecture County from 4.30 to 6.30. Lecture to all officers + NCO's of the B+ts at 6.0 p.m. on 30yds Range.	GWA
"	16/8/18		Collective training for all B+ts from 8.10 to 12.30. C+D B20 on high ground W. of Camp. A+B 2+2 on high ground N.E. of Camp. In the platoon football matches in afternoon B+D 6+2 on Long Range for night firing commencing at 9.15 p.m. A+C B+t on 30yd range for night firing.	GWA
"	17/8/18		Short Range allotted for bath about 8+8 20 during morning. Coy Range A+B with LG during morning. C+D with LG during afternoon. 2nd Lt. OSBORNE + 2nd Lt. McEVOY returned from Div Ldrs this evening during day. Training dull towards end of afternoon.	GWA
"	18/8/18		Service Ancien C of E at 9.15 am R.C. at 9 am in LANNOY Church. R.C Sports took place on footrace ground, went off very well. B+t was G.O. went to dine at Div H.Q. met G.O.C. Servants.	GWA

WAR DIARY or INTELLIGENCE SUMMARY.

6TH LEINSTER REGT Army Form C. 2118.
AUGUST 1916
Sheet VI
VOL XXXVII

Place	Date	Hour	Summary of Events and Information	Remarks and references to Appendices
ABANCOURT	19/8/16		Route March for B[tt]n route ABANCOURT – SECQUEVILLE – FORMERIE – LA GACHIE. G.O.C. met B[tt]n on return, very pleased with the way the men marched. Lt Mullin returned from leave to U.K.	A/A
" "	20/8/16		Collective Training. C & D Coys on high ground with Bayt. A & B Coys on high ground N.E. of Camp. Lewis Gun officer inspected A & B Coys Gas officer lectured Jn all Platoon Officers. Enquiry "Cour d'Enquête" along CRIQUIERS – ABANCOURT Road by O.C. [word] [word] with officer on relieving football match. B[tt]n v 2/2 Northumbrian Field Ambulance. B[tt]n lost 3 – 2.	A/A
" —	21/8/16		Long Range allotted to C Coy from 2 am to 10:30. A & B Coys from 10:30 to 1 whole Bomb Party (219) battn. L.G. class fired on Short range. 1pm whole bomb party (219) battn. L.G. class fired on Short range. all officers & N.C.O.'s L.G. had musketry practise on Short range in enemy from party, 1st of 90 mm, Capt Kavanagh & Lt [Bullen] & Lt Hoy[?] returned from leave to U.K. Lt Carson returned from leave to U.K.	A/A
" —	22/8/16		B[tt]n had use of football ground for training, Brigade Major saw all Coy officers in men at 6 p.m. lectured throughout day. Brigade Major saw all Coy officers in men at 6 p.m. lectured on training etc. Very hot all day	A/A
" —	23/8/16		Individual training. Run bombing course during after noon. Return to begin to Perfumery [Renegard?] early on the Battle of [?] land at 6 p.m. on 30yds range, [worked?] out of the [?] [?] [?] was down at down. weather turned rough in evening.	A/A

WAR DIARY or INTELLIGENCE SUMMARY.

Army Form C. 2118.

6th LEINSTER REGT.

AUGUST 1918. Sheet VII

VOL XXXVII

Place	Date	Hour	Summary of Events and Information	Remarks and references to Appendices
ABANCOURT	24/8/18		Collective Training. A+B Coys on High ground N of Camp C+D Coys on High Ground N.E of Camp. Football Match in afternoon between Bn & 9th Gloucester Regt. Bn 2. Gloucesters 1. Fine throughout day. 2 Pte B. Pope joined Bth having taken commission from the 3 Bn Royal Munster Fus. Capt. J.H. Monaghan returned from leave in Laines.	G.J.H.
—	25/8/18		C of E Service on Gloucesters Regt parade ground. R.C. in church at BLARGIES. ABANCOURT AREA Sports at ABANCOURT. Rev. Mr Ashwell covered party to won 2 events Entertainment given on 30yds range by two officers after entertainment.	R.L.H.
—	26/8/18		Party of 146 sent on Leave today (noted this morning 5=4 N.C.O.'s) 35 of gas officers also took in aspirators listened to all officers of Bn by S.M. gas officer starting their 5.30 to 6.30 a.m. to gas hut. Riding school started at Boulogne to Roulogne 2 Lt Warburton proceeding in charge of Remounts	R.L.H.
—	27/8/18		Schemes on Long Range with Lewis Guns in morning all officers and N.C.O. watched between 8th & 24th Row Park R.E. in enemy at BLARGIES R.E. 1. 8th N.I. 21 Thornton returned from Paris leave. Chauncey all day.	G.J.H.

WAR DIARY
or
INTELLIGENCE SUMMARY.
(Erase heading not required.)

6TH LEINSTER Army Form C. 2118.

AUGUST 1918 Sheet VIII

VOL. XXX VII

Place	Date	Hour	Summary of Events and Information	Remarks and references to Appendices
ABANCOURT	28/8/18		Individual Training carried out. Scheme for all Officers not on Duty. Scheme, outpost duty & pickets. Weather showery all day	N.A.
	29/8/18		Short Range allotted to 1st for day. All employed men fired revolver practice by Officers. No.1 Lewis gunners. Major J. S. Townshend returned from leave to police zone all day. Leathyw noted between 13th to 2/Lt. Mortheman Field Ambulance. 13th 5 – 22th field unit vol. 20 Lewis guns drawing J A.O.D. making Bn up to JC Guns. Battalion found all camp duties. Following Officers reported for duty with Bn 2Lts Inglis H.F. – Mc Gilney J.E. Clark J.J. – Doeling J. Knox A.W.H. – Johnstone J.B. – Bernie R. – Mc Shannon A – Gore J.R. – All come over from England after passing out of Cadet school.	N.A.
	30/8/19		Major Rulong & 2/Lt Knox R. reported their arrival to Bns 2Lt Smyth. 2/Lt O'Neil & 2/Lt Johnstone taken on the strength of Bn 6th Bn Echelon returned from leave in the day. Wet part part of Morning Turning fine later in the day	N.A.
	31/8/15		Weather showery a bit of the month	Appen I

J. Morton Lt.
6 Leinster Rgt

APPX. I

Bttn. Leinster Regt.

Increase.	O.	O.R's.	Decrease.	O.	O.R's
Rejoined Bttn. from Hospital &c.)	-	133.	Sick to Hospital.	-	30.
Joined Bttn. from Base Depôt.)	15.				
	15.	133.			
Decrease.	-	30.			
Net Increase.	15.	103.			

E.M. Harlow Lt.
1/0 Leinster Regt
31-8-16

CONFIDENTIAL.

WAR DIARY

OF

6TH. (S) BN LEINSTER REGT.

From. 1. 9. 18.   To. 16. 9. 18.

Volume No. 37.

WAR DIARY or INTELLIGENCE SUMMARY

(Erase heading not required.)

Army Form C. 2118.

6TH LEINSTER REGT SEPTEMBER 1918   VOL. 37.

Place	Date	Hour	Summary of Events and Information	Remarks and references to Appendices
ABANCOURT	1/9/18		Divine Service. R.C. at BLARGIES Church at 10 A.M. C of E on Lonseuck Regt. parade ground at 9:30 A.M. Football match between Batt. & R.O.D.R.E. at BLARGIES. R.O.D.R.E. v. BLARGIES Bath. 1 R.E. 1.	
"	2/9/18		Short Range allotted to Battn for day – only used during morning owing to Battn being allotted for after noon. All Coys + & Transport Baths.	
"	3/9/18		Battn found all camp duties. Scheme for officers in morning subject "Rear guard" on ABANCOURT – CRIQUIERS Road (DIEPPE Sheet 16) 2nd H.T. Flannery rejoined Battn from Egypt.	
"	4/9/18		Long Range allotted to Battn for day. Fine all day.	
"	5/9/18		Football match between Battn & 2/24th London Regiment. Battn 7 – London 1. "B" Coy had one of their platoons during afternoon – Fine all day.	
"	6/9/18		Short Range allotted to Battn for day. Revolver practice for all officers in evening on Short range. Fine all day.	
"	7/9/18		Scheme for officers in morning. Flank guard (along road LANNOY BOIS DES PLUITS. Sheet 16 DIEPPE) advance guard (along road HODANCOURT – FORMERIE Sheet 16 DIEPPE) Football match in evening between Officers & men – men 5 – officers 1. Fine all day.	
"	8/9/18		Divine Service – R.C. at LANNOY Church 10.0 A.M. C of E on Y.M.C.A Tent at 9.45 A.M.	

Army Form C. 2118.

WAR DIARY 6 LEINSTER REGT.
INTELLIGENCE SUMMARY. SEPTEMBER 1918.
(Erase heading not required.) VOL. 37. ~~XXXVIII~~ Sheet II

Place	Date	Hour	Summary of Events and Information	Remarks and references to Appendices
ABANCOURT	8/9/18		Warning order received at 10.30 pm that the Battalion would be disbanded to reinforce other units of the DIVISION.	JR
	9/9/18		Lt.Col. B.J. JONES. DSO and Capt. Adj. J.H. MONAGHAN. M.C. attended a conference at 198 Infantry Bde.H.Q. to discuss details of disbandment.	JR
	10/9/18		Orders received from 66th DIVN that the disbandment of the Battn would take place forthwith. The following number of other ranks to be transferred). To the 9th Bn Gloucester Regt = 185 (to include 5 Cpls) Enlist personnel. To the 6th Bn Royal Dublin Fus = 105 (to include 5 Cpls) To the 5th Bn Connaught Rangers = 245 (to include 5 Cpls) All classes at Divnl H.Q. schools returned to duty, less 15 signallers being transferred to 5th Conn. Rangers. Orders received to carry out transfers to Gloucesters and Dublin Fusiliers tomorrow. Owing to a number of men being on leave, courses, etc, full allotment of men to be transferred cannot be effected at once.	JR
	11/9/18		The following numbers were available and joined their new units	JR

WAR DIARY 6 LEINSTER REGT.
or
INTELLIGENCE SUMMARY. SEPTEMBER 1918.
Vol. 37. Vol. XXXVIII Sheet III

Army Form C. 2118.

Place	Date	Hour	Summary of Events and Information	Remarks and references to Appendices
ABANCOURT	11/9/18		At 6 p.m. Gloucester Regt = 146 other ranks. Dublin Fus = 96 O.R. The following officers were also transferred: To 6 Dublin Fus = Lieut. W.H. OSBORNE M.C. Lieut C.H. MAGAHY. 2nd Lt L. ATHERTON (now at G.H.Q. Lewis gun school) To 9 GLOUCESTERS = 2nd Lt W.S. BAGNALL 2nd Lieut F. O'NEILL. The Comdg Officer (Lt Col B.J. JONES. DSO) addressed these parties or parade and expressed the hope that they would uphold the best traditions of the Regiment in their new units, before wishing them farewell. The behaviour of the men so excellent. Lt G.E.O. HULLINS and LT W.H. OSBORNE M.C. admitted to F.A. today — the latter not being able to join his new unit. A leave party rejoining last night, a further 21 men joined the 9th Gloucesters and then the 6th Dublin Fus. (18 sick due to Gloucesters and 8 due to Dublins). Lieut A.V. PETRI appointed acting Captain (additional) 14.5.18 :- Authority:— A.G's List No. 203 dated 1.9.18. The Revd F.C. Burns was transferred to the 6th R. Dublin Fus. this day, and the following to the 5th Bn R. Innis Fus :— o/Capt H.E. BRUCE. o/Capt A.V. PETRI. Lieut E.R. SCOTT Lieut G.S. HORTON.	SR
	12/9/18		6 Battalion of 5th Innis. Fus. attached to Batt. pending orders for disposal.	SR

WAR DIARY 6 LEINSTER REGT. Army Form C. 2118.
or
INTELLIGENCE SUMMARY. SEPTEMBER 1918.
(Erase heading not required.) VOLUME 37. Sheet IV.

Place	Date	Hour	Summary of Events and Information	Remarks and references to Appendices
ABANCOURT	13/9/18		Working parties furnished for camp to mt. and a guard over recalled tents of 9th Gloucestin, 5th Innis Fus. Y 6th R.Dublin Fusiliers - these Battns having left AUXI-LE-CHATEAU. Remainder having kits inspected and attending Sun drill. Morning wet, afternoon fine.	JR
—	14/9/18		Musketry on short range and B.F. and P.T. in camp. Revolver practice for Officers on short range. Weather fine with strong wind. Officers played Other ranks at football (Soccer) during the afternoon. Win for O.R. 4 goals to one.	JR
—	15/9/18		Divine Service for R.C.s and C. of E. at BLARGIES. A/Major J.S. TOWNSHEND M.C. ordered to join 6th Lancs. Fus. 199. I. Bde.; to assume duty as 2nd in Command of that Battalion.	JR
—	16/9/18		A.O. 66 Durais notified that the date of disbandment of 6th Batt. Leinster Regt. is the 12th September 1918. War Diary now closes.	JR

J. Murphy Capt.
Leinster Regt.

www.ingramcontent.com/pod-product-compliance
Lightning Source LLC
Chambersburg PA
CBHW081500160426
43193CB00013B/2545